CARROTS LIKE PEAS

and other fun facts

For Mom, who told me carrots
would make my hair grow
—H. E.

For my wife, Lyd's, and daughter, Jack Jack
—A. S.

LITTLE SIMON
An imprint of Simon & Schuster Children's Publishing Division
1230 Avenue of the Americas, New York, New York 10020
This Little Simon Edition November 2015
Series concept by Laura Lyn DiSiena
Copyright © 2015 by Simon & Schuster, Inc.
All rights reserved, including the right of reproduction in whole or in part in any form.
LITTLE SIMON is a registered trademark of Simon & Schuster, Inc., and associated colophon is a trademark of Simon & Schuster, Inc.
For information about special discounts for bulk purchases, please contact Simon & Schuster Special Sales at 1-866-506-1949 or business@simonandschuster.com.
The Simon & Schuster Speakers Bureau can bring authors to your live event. For more information or to book an event contact the
Simon & Schuster Speakers Bureau at 1-866-248-3049 or visit our website at www.simonspeakers.com.
Designed by Ciara Gay
Manufactured in China 0815 SCP
10 9 8 7 6 5 4 3 2 1
This book has been cataloged with the Library of Congress.
ISBN 978-1-4814-3540-6 (pbk) ISBN 978-1-4814-3541-3 (hc) ISBN 978-1-4814-3542-0 (eBook)

CARROTS LIKE PEAS

and other fun facts

By Hannah Eliot

Illustrated by Aaron Spurgeon

LITTLE SIMON

New York   London   Toronto   Sydney   New Delhi

CRUNCH! MUNCH! CHOMP!

Oh, hey there! Have you ever wondered why carrots are orange? It's because they contain beta-carotene. That's the same pigment that's in pumpkins, apricots, nectarines, and other orange fruits and vegetables! Did you know that carrots are a source of vitamin A, which is important for your eyesight? It especially helps you see better at night! Did you know that rabbits actually *don't* eat carrots—that they eat mostly plants and grass? Or that the world's longest carrot was more than 19 feet long?

Really? You knew all of that? Well, did you know that CARROTS LiKE PEAS?

It's true! Carrots and peas help each other grow. This is what's called "companion planting." Companion planting is the practice of planting certain plants near other plants because they help each other. They may keep insects away from each other or produce nutrients that are good for each other.

Sometimes taller plants help by shading smaller plants that wouldn't survive in direct sunlight. Carrots like peas because peas add nitrogen to the soil, helping them grow! Some other examples of companion planting are: grapes and geraniums (the flowers repel beetles from the grapes), sunflowers and lettuce (sunflowers provide the lettuce with shade), and corn and pumpkins (the big pumpkins smother any weeds that might prevent the corn from growing tall)!

Speaking of corn, did you know that the average ear of corn has between 500 and 1,000 kernels on it? The kernels are almost always arranged in an even number of rows—typically 16!

Corn is produced on every continent in the world except for Antarctica. And it's used for many different things. You can find it in plenty of other *foods*, actually. Ice cream, cereals, peanut butter, marshmallows, and chewing gum all contain corn. But so do nonfood items such as soap, glue, fireworks, paint, and more. Wow—that's a lot of uses for corn!

POP! POP! POP!

That popping sound means your popcorn is ready! Would you like to know how popcorn works? Well, each kernel of corn has water inside it. When the kernel is heated, this water turns into steam. Corn kernels have a very hard coating, which makes it difficult for the steam to escape. The steam *eventually* escapes, but it causes the kernel to explode, or pop!

LIGHTS! CAMERA! ACTION!

We've been eating popcorn at the movies since the early 20th century. At that time, however, the movies were still silent. People weren't allowed to bring their popcorn into the theater because it created too much noise! It wasn't until the 1930s that it became acceptable to bring popcorn to the movies. And it only cost about 5 cents a bag!

What else do you like to eat when you go to the movies? Broccoli? Probably not. Spinach? Save that for the dinner table. How about . . . CANDY? Candy dates back to ancient times, when sweet honey taken straight from beehives was a special treat. By definition, candy is made by dissolving sugar in water or milk. This forms a syrup, which is boiled until it starts to caramelize. But we all know there are LOTS of different types of candy.

"How many licks does it take to get to the Tootsie Roll center of a Tootsie Pop?" Haven't you always wondered about the answer to that question? Well, there's no right answer. It's probably best that you just find out for yourself. Did you know that the Tootsie Roll was invented in 1896? Or that it's a chocolate candy that doesn't melt as quickly as *regular* chocolate?

Did you know that no one really knows how jelly beans got their start? Have you heard that Jelly Belly-brand jelly beans were the first ones in OUTER SPACE? That's right! They were on board the 1983 flight of the space shuttle *Challenger*.

Hershey's Kisses were first introduced in 1907. We think that they may have gotten their name because of the sound the machine made when it produced them. It sounded like a kiss!

SMOOCH!

Speaking of chocolate, did you know that more than 36 million heart-shaped boxes of chocolate are sold each year for Valentine's Day? Chocolate has been associated with Valentine's Day for a long time. One of the reasons is that chocolate contains a natural substance called phenylethylamine. A large enough amount of this substance causes changes in blood pressure and blood-sugar levels, leading to feelings of excitement. It also causes your pulse rate to quicken. All of this results in a similar feeling to falling in love!

Can you guess what the most popular ice-cream flavor is? Well, it's not chocolate. It's not pistachio. It's vanilla! What's your favorite flavor? Have you ever eaten it and gotten a BRAIN FREEZE? This happens when cold ice touches the roof of your mouth, causing blood vessels in your head to swell for a moment. The ice-cream cone was supposedly invented in 1904 at the World's Fair in St. Louis. It's thought that an ice-cream vendor didn't have enough bowls, so he teamed up with a waffle vendor, who rolled his waffles into cones!

There have been plenty of cool inventions throughout the history of food. Did you know that Albert Einstein coinvented a refrigerator?

How about the invention of the microwave? That happened when a man named Percy Spencer noticed that the candy bar he had in his pocket had melted as he stood next to radar equipment he was building in a laboratory.

The dishwasher was patented in 1850. That means that no one else could make, use, or sell the same invention. At that time, it was simply a wooden machine that splashed water on dishes when you turned its wheel.

We've been toasting bread since Roman times! The first electric toaster appeared in 1893, and Charles Strite invented the pop-up toaster in 1919. DING! Better go check on that toast!

Speaking of bread, "SANDWiCH" is kind of a funny name, isn't it? Sandwiches got their name because John Montagu, the 4th Earl of Sandwich, used to eat beef between two slices of bread while he was playing cards. This way he could hold his snack in one hand and play cards with the other!

Chips often go along with sandwiches, and they were invented in a funny way too. The story goes:
In 1853, a customer at a restaurant complained that the French fries were too thick. The chef, a man named George Crum, wasn't happy about this. So he cooked paper-thin potatoes until they were way too crisp and sent them out to the customer.
The thing is . . . these "chips" quickly became a favorite!

Flavored chips were introduced in the 1950s, and today they're popular all over the world.

In Britain potato chips are called crisps. Indian chips are often made with exotic spices such as red chili and coriander.

In Germany the most popular flavor is paprika. In Japan, flavors include seaweed and soy sauce!

POTATOES are very starchy vegetables whose plants are usually pollinated by insects such as bees! Some of the potato's best companions are horseradish, beans, marigolds, and peas, because they keep the *bad* insects away.

Potatoes were grown as long ago as 5,000 BC in South America. Around the 13th century they were especially important to the Inca civilization that developed in Peru. Along with being food, they were also thought to help pain, and the Incas placed potato slices on broken bones to help heal them.

Later, potato blossoms were a big hit in royal fashion—Marie Antoinette paraded through the French countryside wearing them!

The Mr. Potato Head doll was born in 1952, and at that time the kit did not come with a potato "body." So customers had to provide their *own* potato into which they could stick the pieces.

And Jelly Belly may have had the first jelly beans taken into outer space, but potatoes were the first food to be *grown* in space! In 1995 potato plants were carried on the space shuttle *Columbia*.

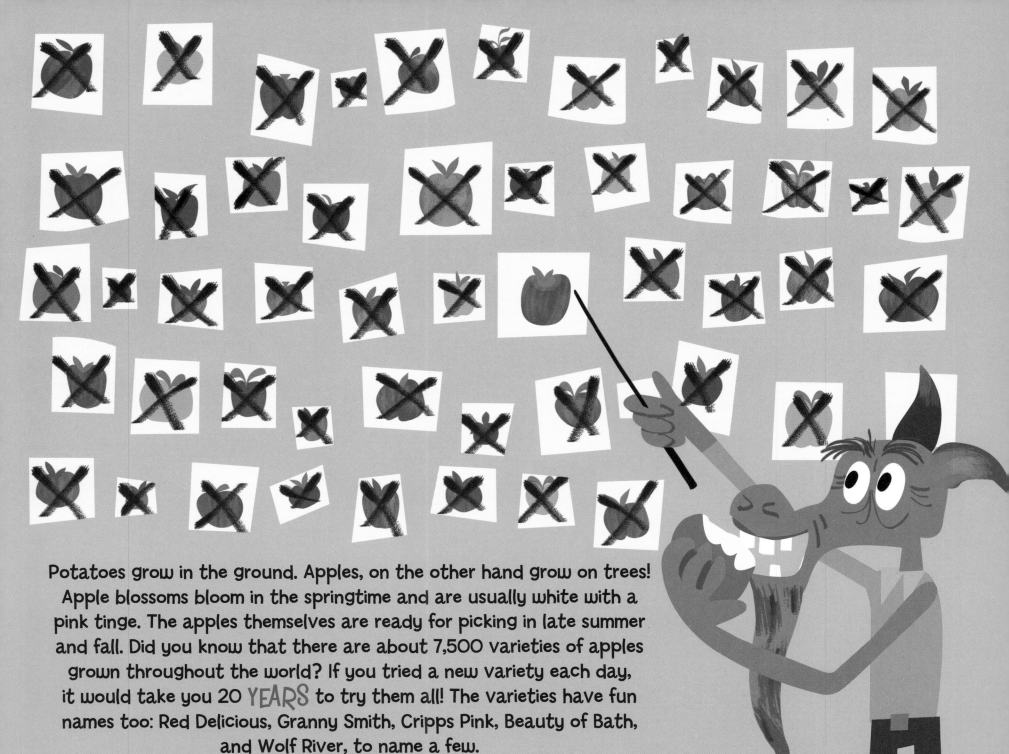

Potatoes grow in the ground. Apples, on the other hand grow on trees! Apple blossoms bloom in the springtime and are usually white with a pink tinge. The apples themselves are ready for picking in late summer and fall. Did you know that there are about 7,500 varieties of apples grown throughout the world? If you tried a new variety each day, it would take you 20 YEARS to try them all! The varieties have fun names too: Red Delicious, Granny Smith, Cripps Pink, Beauty of Bath, and Wolf River, to name a few.

Did you know that the Granny Smith apple was named after the woman
who discovered it in 1868, Maria Ann Smith?
How about that apples float because air pockets inside them make them less dense than water?
Or that apples are a member of the rose family?

What about the saying "An apple a day keeps the doctor away"? Have you ever wondered where that came from? Well, the phrase originated in Wales around 1860, and it went like this: "Eat an apple on going to bed, and you'll keep the doctor from earning his bread." By the early 20th century the saying had evolved into "An apple a day, no doctor to pay." Then it became "An apple a day sends the doctor away." In 1922, the phrase we use now became popular. The truth is, apples are good for you, but it's never been proven that an apple a day actually *does* keep the doctor away!

Is the apple *your* favorite fruit? How about raspberries? A raspberry is actually made up of many TEENY-TINY beadlike fruits called drupelets that surround a core.
Each drupelet has 1 seed, and an average raspberry has 100 to 120 seeds.
Or are you more of a Buddha's hand or dragon fruit person? The BUDDHA'S HAND is sometimes described as a lemon with fingers and was most likely cultivated in China by Buddhist monks.
DRAGON FRUIT is native to Central America but can also be found in Southeast Asia.
It got its name because its skin looks like dragon scales!

There are also lots of fruit-*flavored* foods. Take the Popsicle, for example. Is there anything better on a hot summer day than an ice pop? And it's all thanks to a KID that we have Popsicles! In 1905, 11-year-old Frank Epperson left a cup with a mixture of powdered soda, water, and a stirring stick on his porch. It was a very cold night, and when Frank woke up the next morning, he found a frozen treat! He called this discovery the Epsicle. Later, when he had kids of his own, they always asked for Pop's 'sicle, so he renamed the treat Popsicle!

Pop's EPSICLES for sale

In the 1930s, the owner of the Toll House Inn, Ruth Wakefield, invented the chocolate-chip cookie.

Today, these cookies are one of the most popular kinds! The world's largest chocolate-chip cookie was 102 feet in diameter, weighed 40,000 pounds, and contained 30,000 eggs. WHOA.

DOC'S FAIRY FLOSS

The development of cotton candy might shock you as well. The reason for that is the man who invented it was a dentist! In 1897 he helped invent a machine that heated sugar in a spinning bowl with tiny holes in it. The result was called Fairy Floss—the original name for cotton candy! Today you often see cotton candy at circuses and fairs.

Can you think of another food you'd see at the circus? Peanuts for the elephants? Well, the truth is elephants don't actually like peanuts. The origin of this myth is unknown, but peanuts are still pretty interesting on their own. See, peanuts aren't actually NUTS! They're legumes—the same family that includes beans and lentils.

Did you know that it takes about 540 peanuts to make one 12-ounce jar of peanut butter?
How about that two United States presidents were also peanut farmers: Thomas Jefferson and Jimmy Carter?
Or that the "Elvis" is a sandwich with peanut butter, banana, and bacon? The sandwich got its name because Elvis Presley was known for his love of this exact thing (and also for being a rock-and-roll legend)!

There are 5 places in the United States named Peanut:
Peanut, Arkansas; Peanut, California; and 3 Peanuts in Pennsylvania!

Do you know where pasta was invented? You'd think it was Italy. But in fact, noodles got their start in China!

Today, pasta is one of America's favorite foods. Did you know that there are hundreds of different pasta shapes produced worldwide?

RUOTE
(WHEELS)

STELLINE
(STARS)

FARFALLE
(BOW TIES)

RACCHETTE
(RACKETS)

The first pizzeria, on the other hand, *is* linked to Italy.
You probably order pizza from time to time. Do you know what the top 5 days are for pizza sales? They are Super Bowl Sunday, New Year's Eve, Halloween, the night before Thanksgiving, and New Year's Day!

Both pizza and pasta taste delicious with tomato sauce on them, wouldn't you agree? Did you know that the tomato is a fruit? That's because tomatoes have seeds and grow from a flowering plant.

Have you ever had—or wanted to have—a FOOD FIGHT? Well, the biggest tomato fight in the world happens each year in the Spanish town of Buñol. The festival is called *La Tomatina*, and it usually involves about 30,000 people throwing about 150,000 tomatoes at one another.

Wow, that's a lot of tomatoes! And just like *carrots*, tomatoes—along with corn, cucumbers, eggplant, grapes, okra, parsnips, potatoes, radishes, spinach, strawberries, turnips, and watermelons—like PEAS!

MORE FUN FACTS

Corn: An area in the United States called the corn belt is where the conditions are ideal for growing corn. This area roughly includes Indiana, Illinois, Iowa, Missouri, Nebraska, and Kansas.

Pasta: Black pasta is created by adding squid ink to the dough.

Apples: In order for fruit to grow, apple blossoms need bees or other insects to pollinate them. This is because apples are not self-pollinating.

Pea: "The Princess and the Pea" is a fairytale by Hans Christian Andersen about a princess whose royal identity is tested by whether or not she can feel a pea under a stack of mattresses while sleeping.

Carrot: Carrots are *usually* orange in color, but they can also be purple, red, white, and yellow!

Peanut butter: Arachibutyrophobia is the fear of peanut butter sticking to the roof of one's mouth!

Sandwich: There are lots of names for the sandwich: grinder, hoagie, hero, sub, and more.

Dragon fruit: Dragon fruit grows from a cactus!

Refrigerator: The largest collection of refrigerator magnets in the world is owned by one woman—she has more than 45,000!

Popsicle: Even the ancient Romans had treats similar to Popsicles. They carried blocks of ice down from the mountains in the summer, then crushed the ice and flavored it with fruit and syrup.

Chocolate: The melting point of cocoa butter is just below body temperature, which is why chocolate melts in your mouth!

Potato: Though many Americans include potatoes in their Thanksgiving meal, they were not at the very first Thanksgiving in 1621!

Popcorn: Kernels of popcorn can pop as high as 3 feet into the air!

Candy: A portrait of President Ronald Reagan was once made from 10,000 Jelly Belly beans!